Let's Make Fun
OF THE
FRENCH

Let's Make Fun

OF THE

FRENCH

Edited by
Ima Marakun

Andrews McMeel
Publishing

Kansas City

03 04 05 06 07   BID   10 9 8 7 6 5 4 3 2 1

Bonne chance and special thanks to all contributors!

This book is intended as a work of satire. The opinions expressed in it are not necessarily those of Andrews McMeel Publishing.

ISBN: 0-7407-4093-8

Library of Congress Control Number: 2003109933

Book design by Kelly & Company, Lee's Summit, Missouri

Illustrations by Kevin Brimmer

ATTENTION: SCHOOLS AND BUSINESSES

Andrews McMeel books are available at quantity discounts with bulk purchase for educational, business, or sales promotional use. For information, please write to: Special Sales Department, Andrews McMeel Publishing, 4520 Main Street, Kansas City, Missouri 64111.

Let's Make Fun

OF THE

FRENCH

Charles de Gaulle is
famous for lamenting the
difficulty of governing
a country with 258 varieties
of cheese. Oh, how we
feel for you, Chucky G.

*As far as I'm concerned,
war always means failure.*

Jacques Chirac,
president of France

*As far as France is concerned,
you're right.*

Rush Limbaugh

Q: Where is the best place
to hide your money?

A: Under the soap of a Frenchman.

A French horn is nothing
but a prepubescent tuba.

*The best way to keep one's word
is not to give it.*

Napoleon Bonaparte

Their cheese smells
like people's feet.

During wartime, they huff and puff
and "oui oui" all the way home.

They allowed *Joe Millionaire*
to be taped in their country.

French Country-Western Song

"Don't Cry on My Shoulder 'Cause
You're Messin' Up Mon Hair"

Camembert cheese was originally
known as okay cheese. However,
that name enraged the Department
of Elitism and was changed.

Boy, those French, they have a different word for everything!

Steve Martin

They bottle bathwater
and call it Perrier.

*The French complain of everything,
and always.*

Napoleon Bonaparte

They're far too into
fancy mustard.

Q: What's the thickest
book in a French library?

A: *What to Name Your Cheese.*

Marie Antoinette
makes one smart-ass
remark and gets beheaded.
Nice.

*Raise your right hand
if you like the French. . . .
Raise both hands if you are French.*

—An old saying

French poodles—
enough said.

Their women consider
braided armpit hair a
fashion statement.

Hairstyles include
underarm cornrowing.

French salad dressing
is an obnoxious
orange color.

French drivers
consider pedestrians
hood ornaments.

A fungus by any other
name is a truffle.

You know the French—
smelly and blah, blah, blah.
—Karen on *Will & Grace* after
hanging up on the catty chef
of a trendy French restaurant

LET'S MAKE FUN OF THE **FRENCH**

Q: What do a French military
alliance and a French romance
have in common?

A: Both are brief, sordid,
and completely meaningless.

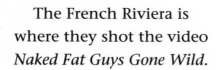

The French Riviera is
where they shot the video
Naked Fat Guys Gone Wild.

They shun McDonald's
but will regularly consume
horsemeat, sheep's feet,
and unrefrigerated cheese.

LET'S MAKE FUN OF THE FRENCH

Q: What do you give
a French man who
has everything?

A: An American
to show him how
to work all of it.

Last Tango in Paris
featured Marlon Brando's
naked butt. Thanks,
I'll sit this one out.

*We can stand here like the French,
or we can do something about it.*

—Marge Simpson

The French Impressionists were
really just a bunch of nearsighted
housepainters trying to make
some extra dough.

The guys have girlie names,
like René.

Q: What is the most useful thing in the French Army?

A: A rearview mirror, so they can see the war.

Only in France would a grown man say, "Ooh la la."

*Years ago, they gave us
the croissant: "le cwa-soh."
And what'd we do?
We turned it into a
"Croissanwich."*

—Denis Leary

French foreign affairs
generally involve
women who don't
even speak French.

Renault
(rhymes with "won't go")
cars.

According to French law,
between the hours of 8:00 A.M.
and 8:00 P.M., 70 percent
of the music on the radio
must be by French composers.

Q: Why did the French celebrate their World Cup Championship in 1998 so wildly?

A: It was the first time they won anything without the help of the United States.

If Napoleon were alive today,
he'd be too short for most
rides at Euro Disney.

Q: Why can't women find a French man
who's sensitive and caring?

A: The French men already
have boyfriends.

In 1886, as a gift symbolizing more than a century of friendship, France gave us the Statue of Liberty; in return, we sent the French eighteen tons of jerky, which they claimed was lost in shipping.

—Dave Barry

They eat frogs' legs.

So they did some cool
stuff during the Renaissance.
Who didn't?

New Orleans's French Quarter
is the last place in America
you'd want your daughter
on a Saturday night.

Imagine how cranky they'd
be *without* all that wine.

*The only way the French are
going in [to war] is if we tell
them we found truffles in Iraq.*
—Dennis Miller

They eat snails.

Do you really expect a country where the boys are named Jacques and Pierre and the war heroes are a teenage girl (Joan of Arc) and a dwarf (Napoleon) to be a military power?

LET'S MAKE FUN OF THE **FRENCH**

Q: How does a French man
plan for the future?

A: He buys two cases of
champagne instead of one.

It's funny that nineteenth-century
French trappers had no qualms
about unilateral war
against America's beavers.

I just love the French.
They taste like chicken.

—Hannibal Lecter

A French rifle is for sale on eBay.
It's described as never been fired,
but dropped once.

French Country-Western Song

"Here's a Franc,
Call Someone Who Cares"

Ah, the allure of French women—
surly attitudes and voluptuous
armpit hair.

Their bread is more
appropriate as a baseball
bat than as food.

The French are big game hunters:
they've been putting snails and frogs'
legs on the dinner table since 1525.

*A lot of folks are still demanding more
evidence before they actually consider
Iraq a threat. For example, France wants
more evidence. And you know I'm
thinking, the last time France wanted
more evidence they rolled right through
Paris with the German flag.*

—David Letterman

It is illegal for French
parents to name a baby girl
Prune, Vanilla, or Cherry.

The Eiffel Tower is the
perfect French monument:
It's extravagant and totally useless.

Donald Rumsfeld was being heckled
by a French antiwar activist when he
suddenly turned and asked the French
man, "Excuse me. Do you speak German?"

The French man replied, "No."

Rumsfeld looked him in the eyes
and said, "You're welcome."

Q: What do you do with a French man who thinks he's God's gift to women?

A: Exchange him.

They gave the world tongue kissing. Oh, wait. That was a good thing.

*I don't know why people are surprised
that France won't help us get Saddam out
of Iraq. After all, France wouldn't help us
get the Germans out of France.*

—Jay Leno

The Louisiana Purchase:
Tough negotiating there,
Mr. Bonaparte.

They take their dogs out to eat
and bring home a "kiddie" bag.

LET'S MAKE FUN OF THE FRENCH

French press coffee—
who wouldn't like their coffee with
a nice mouthful of grounds?

They think croquet is a sport.

They can't quite decide
whether to be snotty or snooty.

Bernard Tapie.

"*Voulez-vous Couchez avec Moi Ce Soir.*"
Crappy pop music, French style.

Broadway producers are saying that because of the war, musicals are suffering from weak ticket sales. Not only that, over at Les Misérables, *the French are refusing to take part in the revolution.*

—Conan O'Brien

*Did you see the new bomb
the government came up with?
It weighs 21,000 pounds. The air force
tested this bomb in Florida, and the
bomb blast was so strong at Disney World
twenty-five French tourists surrendered.*

—Jay Leno

Secret of the French Allure

You're always more charming and
attractive after your fourth glass of wine.

Q: Why are French men like lawn mowers?

A: They emit noxious smells and
half the time they don't work.

In protest of France's opposition to a U.S. war on Iraq, the U.S. Congress's cafeteria has changed "French fries and "French toast" to "freedom fries" and "freedom toast." Afterward, the congressmen were so pleased with themselves, they all started freedom kissing each other.

In a related story, in France, American cheese is now referred to as "idiot cheese."

—Tina Fey, *Saturday Night Live*'s "Weekend Update"

The nickname Frogs isn't
nearly as cool as Yanks.

Gérard Depardieu
or Brad Pitt—
you decide.

Q: What did the president of France say to the German Army as they entered Paris in World War II?

A: Table for 100,000, monsieur?

The French national sport is leapfrog.

French Silk ice cream
makes you fat.

What, they're too good
for sneakers?

They've deluded
gullible street performers
into believing mime is entertaining.

Q: How do you sink a French battleship?

A: Put it in water.

LET'S MAKE FUN OF THE **FRENCH**

A lot of Americans right now are angry at the French. In Washington, the cafeteria where the members of Congress eat announced that they have changed the name of "French fries" to "freedom fries." Nothing like this has happened since the 1950s, when "Russian dressing" changed to "Commie sauce."

—Conan O'Brien

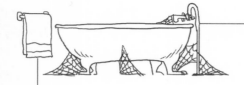

*In France one must adapt
oneself to the fragrance of a urinal.*

—Gertrude Stein

Q: What's the difference between the
French and government bonds?

A: The bonds mature.

French chicks are hot, but
do you know any of them?

*There was another war-related
casualty today. The French
were injured when they tried
to jump on our bandwagon.*

—Jay Leno

Their prolonged obtuse adulation
made Jerry Lewis believe his
films were actually *good.*

*Army personnel in Kuwait unloaded
a dozen faulty tanks that only go in
reverse. Tanks that only go in reverse—
they've been repackaged and sold to France.*

—Craig Kilborn

It's called a *two*-piece swimsuit.
There's a bottom *and* a top.

*France is the only country where
the money falls apart and you
can't tear the toilet paper.*
—Billy Wilder

A French cuff is a boxing match
between angst-ridden poets.

Actual Bumper Sticker

PAVE FRANCE
THE BRITISH NEED MORE PARKING

Everyone agrees that France is just
too nice a country for the French.

Q: What do French and their
wine bottles have in common?

A: They're both empty
from the neck up.

Their national dog is a poodle.

I would call the French scumbags,
but that, of course, would be a
disservice to bags filled with scum.

—Dennis Miller

Pépe Le Pew should have been
charged with sexual harassment.

They get upset when an American
can't pronounce "Eiffel Tower" in French,
but they can't pronounce "please" or
"thank you"—in any language.

What's so romantic
about being on top
of the "Awful Tower"?

Hey, we don't care where the
grapes grew—if it's bubbly wine,
it's called champagne.

Snits 'n' snails 'n'
bunny rabbit tails . . .
that's what the French
are made of.

It took them more than
100 years to finish the
cathedral of Notre-Dame.

*As you know our Allies of Evil are not
being helpful with this Iraqi situation.
With all due respect, I think President Bush
is handling this situation all wrong.
What Bush should do is send someone
the French really respect, like Jerry Lewis.*

—Jay Leno

Actual Bumper Sticker

BOYCOTT FRENCH WHINE

The reason the French talk
through their noses? Garlic.

Le Fries

Q: What are three little words
you'll never hear a
French man say?

A: Can I help?

As far as we know, Louis XIV—
known as le Roi Soleil
(the Sun King)—
never used sunscreen.

You know why the French don't want to bomb Saddam Hussein? Because he hates America, he loves mistresses, and he wears a beret. He is French, people.

—Conan O'Brien

Renault and Peugeot
don't make SUVs.

The French have a word
for arrogant, haughty,
self-important, vainglorious,
and pompous—*moi*.

If *et* is pronounced *ay*,
how do they pronounce *a*?

*President Bush and National Security
Guard Tom Ridge launched the new
Department of Homeland Security,
just twenty-four hours after taking
us down to threat level French—
I'm sorry, I mean threat level yellow.*

—Craig Kilborn

They love their
bread and cheese . . .
American prison food.

French men and French wine—
both are only fit to have dinner with.

Actual Bumper Sticker

FRANCE: IRRELEVANT FOR OVER 150 YEARS

St. Joan is still highly regarded.
After all, she was the last French
virgin to put up a fight.

Let them eat cake.

—Marie Antoinette

Renault? Peugeot? Please.
Give me a good American car
name like Chevrolet or Ford.

After what they say was an exhaustive investigation, the defense minister of France said today that Osama bin Laden is either still in hiding in Afghanistan, he may have escaped to Pakistan, or he may be dead. Hey, France, thanks a lot. We'll take it from here. Hard to believe they were invaded twice.

—Jay Leno

Ahh, the Paris boulevards—
no need for a sewer system.

Q: Why did the French invent
the Foreign Legion?

A: To get their soldiers
the heck outta there.

The French are suspicious of
any foreign influences, like
friendliness or hospitality.

How did
Brigitte Bardot
ever make it
as an actress?
(Hint: Two
big reasons.)

Apparently, they teach their
dogs to poo *on* the sidewalk.

Pablo Picasso went through
his "Blue Period" after
moving to France.

They put in only
thirty-five-hour workweeks.

In Hungary, one of the most
common swearwords, used in
cinema subtitles to translate
pretty much anything
obscene in English, is
"a Francba!" It means
roughly "go to France!"

A Cross Between Greenpeace and the French: "Save the whales, eat the snails."

French Country-Western Song

"I Don't Know Whether to Kill Myself or Have a Moët"

*We at the French's Company wish to put
an end to statements that our product
is manufactured in France. There is no
relationship, nor has there ever been
a relationship, between our mustard
and the country of France. Indeed, our
mustard is manufactured in Rochester,
New York. The only thing we have in
common is that we are both yellow.*

—Statement by the makers
of French's mustard

It is impossible to
wear a beret without
looking like a complete fool.

Pickpocketing accounts for
50 percent of the French GNP.

They turn their evil dictators
into puff pastry.

Unfortunately,
Paris is full of French people.

When's the last time a French
man won the Tour de France?

Their greatest attraction
is a glorified radio tower.

LET'S MAKE FUN OF THE FRENCH

*French troops arrived in Afghanistan
last week, and not a minute too soon.
The French are acting as advisers
to the Taliban, to teach them how
to surrender properly.*

—Jay Leno

*Late Show with
David Letterman*

**Top Ten Ways France
Is Celebrating Their
World Cup of Victory**

10. A good old-fashioned poodle roast.

9. French-kissing the guy who yells,
   "Gooooaaaaalllll!!!"

8. Surrendering to Germany.

7. Dousing coach with
   tub of melted Brie.

LET'S MAKE FUN OF THE **FRENCH**

6. Being thankful that they finally won something without begging the United States for help.

5. Getting le faced.

4. Carrying around signs reading, "See? We're not as fruity as you think we are."

3. Ticker-tape parade inside President Jacques Chirac's nostrils.

2. Commemorating the rarity of this occasion by taking showers.

1. "I'm going to Euro Disney World!"

French toast actually tastes
best when it's made from
all-American Texas toast.

Q: What do you call a French
man with a vasectomy?

A: A humanitarian.

They intended to have the Statue of Liberty
full of French troops à la the Trojan Horse
but chickened out at the last minute.

*What do you expect from a culture and
a nation that exerted more of its national
will fighting against Disney World and
Big Macs than the Nazis?*
—Dennis Miller

They make their dogs
look like sissies.

Most small servings of fast-food
French fries contain about 220 calories.

They picked a rooster
(cock) for their emblem.

I'm sure there is a Frenchman who can crack a decent joke, but I have yet to meet him. The sad truth is that the French have no discernible sense of humor. They laugh from time to time it is true, but this only occurs when they see a magnificent menu or they are being paid. As more and more Frenchmen now dine at Quickburger, and unemployment rises, you can now go for days on end in many parts of France without hearing so much as a titter.

—Denise Thatcher,
France: The Final Days

Kansas City, Missouri,
has more fountains than Paris.

You know what they say . . .
little cars, little dogs.

*The French probably invented the
very notion of discretion. It's not
that they feel that what you don't
know won't hurt you, they feel that
what you don't know won't hurt them.
To the French lying is simply talking.*

—Fran Lebowitz

"French" fries were
actually invented
in Belgium.

Their greatest
invention
is the bidet.

Jewel of the French
Catholic Firmament

St. Geneviève—Saved Paris
from Attila the Hun
(Where was she when
Disney came to town?)
—Denise Thatcher,
France: The Final Days

French men adore
dating married women—
unless the women
are their wives.

They apparently
never got around to
finishing the Eiffel Tower.

To err is human.
To loaf is Parisian.

—Victor Hugo

"Arrogance."
That's French,
right?

Q: What do you call a French man who's faithful?

A: Impotent.

Seminar for French Men

His Wife Can Be Yours, Too

LET'S MAKE FUN OF THE **FRENCH**

Serge Gainsbourg
was an old letch.

The problem with French food
is that you're snotty again
in five minutes.

*Tomorrow is Bastille Day,
the French July Fourth.
This is the day when the
French peasants declared
that they—not just their aristocratic
overlords—had rights. They too had the
right to: serve salad after you've already
eaten a whole meal; serve cheese after
you've just eaten a salad you didn't want to
eat in the first place; wear a black turtleneck
even though it is quite hot outside and you
haven't bathed for at least a few days.*

—Jonah Goldberg, nationalreview.com

LET'S MAKE FUN OF THE **FRENCH**

They celebrate a holiday
known as Prison Day.

*The objects of which Paris
folks are fond: literature, art,
medicine, and adultery.*
—Mark Twain

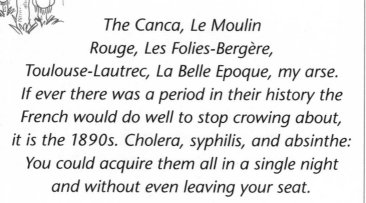

*The Canca, Le Moulin
Rouge, Les Folies-Bergère,
Toulouse-Lautrec, La Belle Epoque, my arse.
If ever there was a period in their history the
French would do well to stop crowing about,
it is the 1890s. Cholera, syphilis, and absinthe:
You could acquire them all in a single night
and without even leaving your seat.*

—Denise Thatcher,
France: The Final Days

LET'S MAKE FUN OF THE **FRENCH**

Q: Why do French men watch soccer?

A: Because it's dull talking about
sex every waking moment.

A la mode translated
means "in fashion."
What's this have
to do with
ice cream?

*"Voulez que je vous porte
au mall dans mon SUV?"*
(Want me to take you to
the mall in my SUV?)

—Dave Barry

Marcel Marceau.

They push stuff that pigs sniff
and call it "gourmet."

*Europe saw one of the biggest
meteor showers in history.
Everyone in France was excited
and wanted to know,
"What's a shower?"*

—Conan O'Brien

World Cup 1998:
Hosted it. Won it.
Nice manners!

Instead of having muscles,
they *eat* mussels.

*A Frenchman's home is
where another man's wife is.*

—Mark Twain

The *New York Post* branded
France and Germany
the "Axis of Weasel."

Late Show with
David Letterman

**Top Ten Insulting French
Nicknames for Paul Shaffer**

10. Le Petit Piano Monkey

9. Hunchback of Notre-Lame

8. Le Canadian Weasel

7. Mon Petit Shaf-Shaf

6. Le Dork de Triomphe

5. Gérard Depardon't

4. Charles de Balde

3. The Eiffel Loser

2. The Inventor of the
Flesh-Colored Beret

1. Crepe-y

*In Cognac . . .
you stand out if
the end of your nose
does not resemble
a red golf ball.*

—Denise Thatcher,
France: The Final Days

Secret of the French Allure

Eat enough raw garlic and
you'll be as sexy as an Italian.

"A la carte" is a silly
way to order a meal.

They're none
too friendly to
the hunchbacked.

A fool needs neither bell nor
bauble; his words and actions
quickly will speak for him.
—French proverb

American soldiers say, "Don't
shoot until you see the whites
of their eyes." French soldiers say,
"If you see the whites of their eyes,
you should have surrendered."

They invented "etiquette,"
so why are they so rude?

*After a man hath drunk
hard he dare anything.*

—French proverb

French must be an easy
language to learn. If the
French can speak it,
how hard can it be?

*Although it was popular
in the rest of the world,*
Psycho *was banned in France
for fear it might inspire
copycat showers.*

—Craig Kilborn

You can't make a decent size
sandwich with a baguette.

Timex keeps just as good
as time as Cartier—for a
few thousand dollars less.

*Children of primary school age
find wine in their lunchboxes.*

—Denise Thatcher,
France: The Final Days

LET'S MAKE FUN OF THE FRENCH

Seminar for French Men

Bad Wine versus
the End of the World:
What's the Difference?

French filmzzzzz . . .

Wine wears no breeches;
a drunkard conceals nothing.

—French proverb

Hygiene does not seem
to be their top priority.

Q: What do you call a
Frenchman in the trenches?

A: Lost.

French resistance in
World War II was legendary . . .
all three days of it.

One might plausibly argue, indeed, that the complete disappearance of France would produce no more perturbation in the world than the loss of an ear produces in a man. Brussels and Lucerne would quickly put in better cooks, and Copenhagen, I venture, could take care of the peep-show business without any need of an international loan.

—H. L. Mencken's editorial in the *American Mercury,* April 1927

Here's your "tip":
Next time, try being nicer!

A Louis Vuitton purse costs more
than most small European cars.

Many French people believe
smoking is an adequate
substitute for bathing.

When Charles de Gaulle decided to retire from public life, the British ambassador and his wife threw a gala dinner party in his honor. At the dinner table the ambassador's wife was talking with Madame de Gaulle.

"Your husband has been such a prominent public figure, such a presence on the French and international scene for so many years! How quiet retirement will seem in comparison. What are you most looking forward to in these retirement years?"

LET'S MAKE FUN OF THE FRENCH

"A penis,"
replied Madame de Gaulle.

A huge hush fell over the table.
Everyone heard her answer,
and no one knew what to say next.

Le Grand Charles leaned over to
his wife and said, "Ma chérie,
I believe ze English
pronounce zat
word 'appiness'!"

In Cognac you are considered drunk only if you are unable to raise your glass.

—Denise Thatcher,
France: The Final Days

Seminar for French Men

Crying and Marching

*François Truffaut is an
Alfred Hitchcock wannabe.*

Jean-Luc Godard is a
François Truffaut wannabe.

The earliest remains of *Homo sapiens* were found at Cro-Magnon in France. Some believe many Cro-Magnons still live in France.

They economize by using one toothbrush per family.

*France is a dog hole, and it no more
merits the tread of a man's foot.*

—William Shakespeare,
All's Well That Ends Well

Foie gras: Goose liver + pork fat
+ onions. Yum-yum!

Well, they *have* solved the
secondhand smoke problem:
If everyone smokes, there
are no secondhand smokers.

Q: How many French men does
it take to change a lightbulb?

A: One. He holds the bulb and all
of Europe revolves around him.

LET'S MAKE FUN OF THE FRENCH

Rococo.
Has anybody in France ever
heard that less is more?

No matter how much
we insult them,
they refuse to
change the
name of
American cheese.

A strange chap called President Chirac

Was well known for knocking the Kir back

He'd get a few belts in

With President Yeltsin

Then of comrades acknowledge
the sheer lack.

—Denise Thatcher, *France: The Final Days*

Seminar for French Men

You Can Do Your Hair
in Less Than Four Hours

Napolean's penis is preserved
in a jar. A very small jar.

Q: How many Frenchmen does it take to defend Paris?

A: Nobody knows, it's never been tried.

There's all that air kissing.

They look like Johnny Holliday.

*The only time France wants
us to go to war is when the
German Army is sitting in
Paris sipping coffee.*
—Regis Philbin

Bouillabaisse:
Hard to spell, even harder to eat.

What can you say about
a nation with 200 cheeses
and one kind of toilet paper?

LET'S MAKE FUN OF THE **FRENCH**

Q: Why don't they have
fireworks at Euro Disney?

A: Because every time they shoot
them off, the French try to surrender.

France: where Mary is hairy
and Nelly is smelly.

*When the final nail is driven home
into the coffin of France it will be
by a hammer wielded by one of
Walter Elias Disney's seven dwarfs.
Which one am I thinking of . . . Crappy,
Greedy, Schmaltzy, Yukkie, Sniffy,
Barmy, or Grotty? Take your pick.*

—Denise Thatcher,
France: The Final Days

French K rations
include three wines to
go with running shoes.

Seminar for French Men

The Seven-Hour Workweek

Their perennial best-seller
is *I'm OK, You're Not.*

Q: Why did the French plant trees
along the Champs-Elysées?

A: So the Germans could
march in the shade.

The French view us as a bunch of fat, simplistic, SUV-driving, gum-chewing, gun-shooting, mall-dwelling, John Wayne cowboys who put ketchup on everything we eat, including breath mints. Whereas we view the French as a bunch of snotty, hygiene-impaired, pseudo-intellectual, snail-slurping weenies whose sole military accomplishment in the past 100 years was inventing the tasseled combat boot.

—Dave Barry

*Late Show with
David Letterman*

**Top Ten Ways to Make the
Tour de France More Exciting**

10. Let spectators vote to "banish"
competitor with sissiest shorts

9. Only one bicycle:
fight over who gets to ride it

8. Place last in Stage 12, must ride
Stage 13 without bicycle seat

7. Day 3: Release the Dobermans!

6. Good-bye Gatorade,
hello Jack and Coke

5. No finish line. Winner is last guy
to collapse from exhaustion.

4. Move it to that navy bombing
range in Puerto Rico

3. Make 'em take enough steroids
to ride 500 miles an hour

2. Here's all you need to make
it exciting: Anna Kournikova

1. Make it the
Tour de South Bronx

Face it, they've been
creatively outdone with
the red, white, and blue.

Louis XIV—
a king so good he
became a furniture style.

Oil can be refined
without being arrogant.

Q: How many gears does
a French tank have?

A: Four reverse and one
forward, in case the enemy
attacks from the rear.

But the fact that we hate each other, with good reason, does not mean we can't be friends! After all, the United States and France have a close relationship that dates back to the Revolutionary War, when we were helped in our struggle for independence by a French person whose name we

*will never, ever forget, as long as
we have Internet access to the*
Encyclopaedia Britannica.
According to the Encyclopaedia
Britannica, *his full name was—
I am not making this up—Marie-
Joseph-Paul-Yves-Roch-Gilbert du
Motier, Marquis de Lafayette.*

—Dave Barry

Their idea of an exercise plan
is jogging back to the bakery
for more cream-filled pastries.

The new French national anthem
should be "Born to Run."

Seminar for French Men

Advanced Driving: How You Can
Do 100 Miles Per Hour in Rush Hour
Without Nicking the Arc de Triomphe

Guillotines—
now that's abrupt!

Q: How can you identify a French infantryman?

A: Sunburned armpits.

They think they carry a lot of weight in world affairs, whereas in reality they just carry a lot of weight.

*Finally, this week the
French soldiers have showed
up in Afghanistan. Figures—
just like the French to show up after
the hard work has been done.*

—Jay Leno

Charles de Gaulle . . .
a president, a philanderer,
an airport.

Navigating around the
Arc de Triomphe would
drive *anyone* crazy.

Q: What's the difference
between French men and toast?

A: You can make soldiers out of toast.

René Descartes created
analytical geometry.
Gee, we were wondering
who to thank for all
that math homework.

They have no such thing as
a beer belly; they call it (and
this is the best translation),
"My Best Buddy."

The French machine gun
should be known
as Old Yeller.

*We had the good taste
to chisel the armpit hair
off the Statue of Liberty you
gave us. You know something,
I always thought that tint was
oxidized copper. Little did I know
it was green with envy.*

—Dennis Miller

Jewel of the French
Catholic Firmament

St. Louis—The only French king to have been canonized. Has spent the last 1,000 years trying to disprove the adage "No man is an island."

—Denise Thatcher,
France: The Final Days

French is Miss Piggy's
favorite language.

Q: What do you call 100,000
Frenchmen with their hands up?

A: The army.

The French contributed silly phrases
to American linguistic culture like
joie de vivre, cause célèbre, and
pièce de résistance.

Really—is there any way to
drink Dom Pérignon without
being pretentious?

He had a hellish childhood. His mother would lean out the kitchen window and shout: "Marie-Joseph-Paul-Yves-Roch-Gilbert du Motier, Marquis de Lafayette! You get back in here and finish your snails this instant!"

—Dave Barry

Merci—
the only French word
American tourists know,
but one they'll never hear.

Compared to a French film,
On Golden Pond is action-packed.

Q: Why wouldn't the
Statue of Liberty
work in France?

A: Because she has
only one arm raised.

Going to war without France is like going deer hunting without your accordion.

—Norman Schwartzkopf

The proper way to use a French bayonet:
(1) cheese skewer; (2) fondue fork;
(3) holding up a white flag.

If the French are so sexually liberated,
why do they have to hide behind the
coy phrase "au naturel" instead
of just saying "buck naked"?

Seminar for French Men

High-Stakes World Politics:
Deal Yourself Out

They refuse to smile because
they've got snails caught in their teeth.

Q: How do you stop a French tank?

A: Say "boo."

"Voulez-vous la gomme?
Elle ketchup-est assaisonnee!"
(Do you want gum?
It's ketchup-flavored!)

—Dave Barry

Appropriately,
French words found
in the English language
include *divorce, nonchalant,*
and *critique.*

More appropriately,
French words also found
in the English language
include *exposé*, *cliché*,
and *façade*.

Jacques Cousteau
inspired the annoying
John Denver song "Calypso."

The closest they've ever come
to a good outdoor barbecue
involved Joan of Arc.

The French Army theme song:
"Be Our Guest! Be Our Guest!"

They have a national
Be-Rude-to-Foreigners-Day,
which is celebrated year-round.

*Two things a
drunkard does disclose,
a fiery face and crimson nose.*

—French proverb

Seminar for French Men

Soccer: Not a Game—a Sacrament

Their method for taking care
of body odor is really
fast bicycle riding.

Q: Why do the French
get more votes in the UN?

A: They vote with both hands.

Their idea of Super Sized is a
"tide-me-over-till-we-eat" snack.

France has neither winter nor summer nor morals. Apart from these drawbacks it is a fine country. France has usually been governed by prostitutes.

—Mark Twain

Croissant . . . baguette . . .
neither will fit in a toaster.

One of their most famous novels,
Les Misérables, is 1,500 pages about
some guy who stole a loaf of bread.

Q: How do you get Americans to stop buying cigarettes?

A: Put a picture of a French guy on the box.

Not only was Napoleon
Bonaparte the smallest
dictator in history but he
also had a really hairy back.

They charge you more money the
higher up you go in the Eiffel Tower.

*I would rather have a German
division in front of me than
a French one behind me.*

—General George S. Patton

Seminar for French Men

To Love, Honor, and Cherish:
Remembering the Small Print Above "I Do"

The French National Security Agency
consists of a roving band
of yappy little dogs.

When the French sneeze, it sounds
like they're yelling profanity.
You don't know whether
to say "Gesundheit!" or
"What'd you call my mother?"

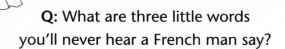

Q: What are three little words
you'll never hear a French man say?

A: Make mine Velveeta.

Forget the Dannon and Yoplait—
we'll take just plain ice cream.

In politics . . . never retreat, never retract, never admit a mistake.

—Napoleon Bonaparte

Q: What is a popular American movie in France?

A: *The Running Man.*

The entire country goes on
vacation in August as a national
annual prank on tourists.

The name of their country
rhymes so well with *underpants*.

LET'S MAKE FUN OF THE FRENCH

Q: Why don't cheeseburgers
sell well in France?

A: Because they don't
smell like cheese.

A movie and dinner
date is called
an "Artsy Fartsy."

*You know, the French
remind me a little bit of
an aging actress of the
1940s who was still trying
to dine out on her looks but
doesn't have the face for it.*

—John McCain,
U.S. senator from Arizona

Q: Why do French men have mustaches?

A: To remind them of their mothers.

Seminar for French Men

Beyond Clean and Dirty:
How Apache Shirts Hide
Those Nasty Snail Stains

They're still cursing the
invention of margarine.

Q: When is it white laundry day in France?

A: Never. Any white laundry in France is
already hung up on a stick being waved.

They've always regretted not giving
us a nice greeting card instead
of the Statue of Liberty.

Claude Monet had cataracts—
that explains the fuzzy imagery.

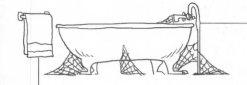

*In politics, an absurdity
is not a handicap.*

—Napoleon Bonaparte

Chanel No. 5—how bad
did the first four batches smell?

For such a fashion-conscious people,
they've designed a really boring flag.

Q: Why don't MasterCard and Visa
work well in France?

A: They do not know how
to say *"Charge!"*

The phrase
"Say it, don't spray it"
was conceived there.

Q: At what age does a French
boy reach maturity?

A: Forty-five—or when his mommy
throws him out of the château.

They think the height of chic
is Jean Paul Gaultier.

Sadly, all Frenchmen
are created equal.

French royalty were
notorious perverts.

You'll never hear anyone yell,
"Show me the Monet!"

French cartoonists weren't
even nice about the
Columbia shuttle disaster.

Really—what's the big deal
about the *Mona Lisa*?

The few non-French people
who actually think berets
look cool include
Monica Lewinsky and
Saddam Hussein.